DATE DUE

OCT 04

GAYLORD			PRINTED IN U.S.A.

The Inuit

Suzanne M. Williams

Franklin Watts
A Division of Scholastic Inc.
New York • Toronto • London • Auckland • Sydney
Mexico City • New Delhi • Hong Kong
Danbury, Connecticut

To the Inuit elders and the children who learn from them

Note to readers: Definitions for words in **bold** can be found in the Glossary at the back of this book.

Photographs © 2003: Alison Wright Photography: 31, 40; Arctic Winter Games: 42; Bridgeman Art Library International Ltd., London/New York: 29 (Private Collection); Bryan and Cherry Alexander: 3 left, 4, 6, 15, 16, 33, 34, 39, 41; Corbis Images: 32 (Bettmann), 17 (Roger Ressmeyer); Network Aspen/David Hiser: 8 top, 8 bottom, 18, 22, 37 top, 37 bottom; North Wind Picture Archives: 26; Peter Arnold Inc./Fred Bruemmer: 3 right, 13; Photo Researchers, NY: 38 (Stephenie Hollyman), 10 (Ted Kerasote), 9 (SPL); The Image Works/Eastcott-Momatiuk: 24; TRIP Photo Library/ N Price: 45; Woodfin Camp & Associates/Eastcott-Momatiuk: 20.

Cover illustration by Gary Overacre based on a photo from Corbis Images by Michael Maslan, Historic Photographs.

Map by XNR Productions Inc.

Poem on page 23:
Copyright ©1971 by Richard Lewis
First appeared in I BREATHE A NEW SONG, POEMS OF THE ESKIMO, published by Simon & Schuster. Reprinted by permission of Curtis Brown, Ltd.

Library of Congress Cataloging-in-Publication Data

Williams, Suzanne M. 1949–
    The Inuit / by Suzanne M. Williams.
        p. cm. — (Watts library)
    Summary: A look at the history and culture of the Inuit, a group of Native American people who live in the Arctic, discusses tradition and customs as well as contemporary life.
    ISBN 0-531-12172-0 (lib. bdg.)   0-531-16235-4 (pbk.)
    1. Inuit—Juvenile literature. [1. Inuit. 2. Eskimos.] I. Title. II. Series.
E99.E7W724 2003
971.9004'9712—dc21

2003003991

Contents

An Inuit man pulls a cod fish from the water.

Chapter One

Arctic People

The motor of the gas-powered auger roars. Ice flies. The fisherman quickly cuts a deep round hole in the sea ice. It's not deep enough. The ice on Canada's Hudson Bay is more than 7 feet (2.13 meters) thick. It is May. The fisherman switches to Inuit traditional tools to finish. His mother settles by the hole to fish for bass or arctic char. Children play nearby.

An Inuit Family

This family is Inuit, the native people who live on the edge of Hudson Bay. Life has changed quickly for the Inuit. Grandparents, parents, and children have had

An Inuit family enjoys a meal on the tundra during a summer hunting trip.

very different experiences. Like most older Inuit, the grandparents in this family speak in an Inuit language, **Inuktitut**. They were born when Inuit lived by moving around, hunting and gathering. Inuit call this "living on the land." The oldest Inuits, or **elders**, remember the traditional life of seal hunting in the winter, whaling in spring, and following caribou in the summer. Many of them were adults before they moved to Canadian settlements.

Many older women, like this grandmother, make beautiful **parkas** and *kamiit*, waterproof animal-skin boots, for their

Inuit and Eskimo

Inuit means "people" in Inuktitut. Another English word for Inuit is Eskimo. Today, "Eskimo" is an insulting word in Canada. However, in Alaska, many Yup'ik and Inupiat people, who are closely related to the Inuit, call themselves Eskimos. Older books, materials about Alaska, and the names of some Canadian companies and organizations that were formed years ago still use the word Eskimo.

families. The grandfather tells stories about ancestors, magic animals, and adventure. Sometimes he plays **string games** with the children as he talks. The string figures match his stories!

Most middle-aged Inuit speak English and Inuktitut. They may work for the government, at schools, or in businesses. Sometimes adults carve stone sculptures, make art prints, or sew clothing to sell to tourists and art galleries.

Like many Inuit their age, the mother and father never lived full time on the land. They learned Inuktitut at home and English in a government school. The family lives in a small house, and the parents drive a snowmobile when they hunt or visit friends. It is faster and cheaper than keeping dogs and a dogsled, the way their parents did. Most younger Inuit adults learned the Inuit ways of hunting and fishing from their parents. They know the stories and dances. They use **southern** things to make their life easier.

The children go to school. They learn in both English and Inuktitut. Sometimes elders, like the grandparents, come to school to tell stories or teach sewing. Grandfather teaches about the stars and making mental maps to get from place to place on the land. The elders want Inuit children to learn the traditional ways of living in the Arctic.

North and South

In northern Canada, people and things from the Canadian, European, and American cultures are called southern.

The Arctic: an Extreme Challenge

It takes skill to live in the Arctic. Snow blows across the frozen ground. It blends into the sky. The temperature hangs near 0° Fahrenheit (-18° Celsius). It is spring.

Animals emerge from burrows. Caribou will drop their calves, and whales will **migrate** to their summer homes. The top few inches of **tundra** will thaw. Sea ice begins to warm.

The arctic world is extreme. Above the Arctic Circle, the sun may disappear for weeks in midwinter. It may shine for weeks in midsummer without getting dark. Winter temperatures may drop below -40°F (-40°C). Yet summer days can be very warm. The Arctic is usually covered with snow, ice, and frozen seawater, but little rain or snow falls. Most of the arctic Canadian territory, **Nunavut**, receives less than 11.8 inches (300 millimeters) of **precipitation** in a year.

In the summer, the surface of the soil thaws, but several inches down is **permafrost**, ground that is always frozen.

Polar bears are only some of the animals that make the Arctic their home.

Tundra plants grow during the short summers. The flat land and the permafrost combine to make drainage poor.

Few plants and animals can live here. No trees grow here. Arctic animals **adapted** to their surroundings. Arctic foxes and hares grow white fur in the winter to match the snow. Beluga whales use a hard ridge on their back to break ice so that they can breathe. Whales and seals have thick layers of fat, **blubber**, to keep them warm. Some animals migrate. They walk or fly to the warmer south in the winter. Others **hibernate**, sleeping through the winter in warm burrows.

People learned to live here too. The Inuit's ancestors arrived thousands of years ago. They learned skills to live in the Arctic. They learned to stay warm when it was -65°F (-53.8°C), and to travel miles across snow and ice to hunt. They made games for the long nights. Today Inuit teach their children how to live on their special land. Their stories pass on the knowledge that makes living in the Arctic possible. They tell the history of Inuit people.

Arctic Days and Nights

Imagine that Earth is a ball twirling on a flagpole. The Sun shines at it from the side. Half the ball is shadowed, and half is lit. Day and night change as a place on Earth turns toward the Sun (day) or away from the Sun (night).

However, Earth doesn't spin on an upright stick. It **rotates**, or turns, around an imaginary line, its **axis**. The axis is tilted. The tilted, spinning earth travels around the Sun once each year. As it moves, the seasons and the length of day and night change.

In June and July, the North Pole is tilted toward the Sun. The Sun doesn't set for weeks. In December and January, the North Pole points away from the Sun, which means there are many weeks of darkness.

According to Inuit legend, Atunga and his wife left their homelands to travel around the world on foot.

Chapter Two

Travelers and Hunters

One Inuit legend says a man named Atunga and his wife decided to walk around the world. They left their young daughter at home. They traveled by dog-sled and boat. They even passed through the land of the *qallunaat*, or white people, where they got beads for their daughter. After many years, they returned home. Their daughter was old, but the travelers were still young. The daughter laughed at the beads, saying, "What will an old woman do with beads?"

Closely Related

Yup'ik and Inupiat people live in Alaska. Inuvialuit people live in the northern Yukon. Different groups of Inuit live in the central and eastern Canadian Arctic. Others live in Greenland. Yup'ik, Inupiat, Inuvialuit, and Inuit people understand each other's languages. They have similar traditions.

Traveling to a New Land

Look down at the top of a globe. Northern Europe, Asia, North America, and Greenland form a ring around the North Pole. Today about 150,000 Inuit live across more than half of this circle. Like Atunga, Inuit ancestors trekked, from Alaska across North America to places as far away as Greenland and Labrador.

The Inuit weren't the first people in the Arctic. At least 12,000 years ago, people from Asia followed herds of caribou and mammoth north and east. They hunted the animals for food and clothing. At that time, much of Earth's water was frozen in glaciers and ice sheets. The sea level was lower. People and animals could walk from Siberia in Asia, to Alaska in North America. They probably crossed the **Bering Land Bridge**, or Beringia.

Most of those early travelers passed through the cold, treeless Arctic. They spread throughout North and South America. They were ancestors of today's American Indians.

About 11,000 years ago Earth warmed, ice melted, and sea level rose. Ocean water flooded the land bridge. Still, more

Arctic Small Tool Tradition

The people of the **Arctic Small Tool tradition** may have come from Siberia in northeast Asia. They made very small, sharp spear points, scrapers, and carving tools. Many of their tools were only about 2 inches (5 centimeters) long. The tools are often found at ancient campsites, near rings of stones that probably held the sides of skin tents. These sites are found in many places across the Arctic.

people came from Asia. No one is sure how they traveled to North America. They may have crossed the Bering Sea in boats or crossed on sea ice in winter.

Archaeologists have found evidence of **Paleo-Arctic people** living along Alaska's coastline and in the Yukon between 8000 and 5000 B.C. They have found fine stone tools of people from the Arctic Small Tool tradition (2200–800B.C.) across Alaska and the Canadian Arctic.

By about 500 B.C., **Dorset** people, in the Canadian Arctic, hunted large animals such as walruses and seals on the sea ice. They made delicate carvings. About the same time, **Thule** people, in Alaska, were learning to hunt whales and walruses from boats in open water. The Thule tamed and trained dogs to pull sleds. In the summer, they traveled from place to place, living in skin tents. They hunted caribou and other animals. They spent winters in villages of sod houses built with whalebone rafters. Around A.D. 1, they began moving east across the Arctic, creating new communities as they traveled.

This is a reconstruction of a Thule house.

13

Igloos, Sod Houses, and Tents

The word for "house" in Inuktitut, is *iglu* (igloo). Sod, snow, and wooden houses are all called *igluit* (igloos). Snow igloos can also be made of ice blocks or have a skin roof, depending on the weather and the materials that are available. Skin tents, used in the summer, are called *tupiit* (one is a *tupiq*).

When Thule people lived in villages, they built permanent sod houses that they used in winter. As the climate got colder in later centuries, Yup'ik, Inupiat, and some Inuvialuit people continued to live, part time, in sod houses. Sometimes they built snow houses when they traveled in the winter. Inuit people in the central and eastern Arctic had a harder time finding food on the barren tundra. They moved more often, spending much of the winter in snow houses.

By A.D. 1000, Thule people had spread from Alaska to Greenland. Perhaps the Dorset people had moved away, or began living like their new Thule neighbors. Signs of the Dorset culture disappeared.

About 1500, the climate changed. Colder winters made it harder to support many people in winter villages. Some Thule people began to move in both summer and winter. If they kept moving, there was enough game to eat. In the winter they built temporary snow shelters—**igloos**. In the summer they lived in skin tents. The Thule changed their way of life. Now they were Inuit.

Inuit call the early arctic people **Tuniit**. They say Tuniit were giants who didn't like to fight. When Inuit came to their land, they just ran away. Tuniit could change into animals, and, in their time, animals could become people.

Hunters' Skills

From earliest times, arctic people hunted caribou and musk oxen. They quietly tracked the herds and shot animals with arrows. Sometimes hunters built big stone figures that looked like people—*inuksuit*. They put moss and leaves on the stones to look like hair. When caribou saw the *inuksuit* they went the other way, toward the hiding hunters!

Dorset, Thule, and Inuit people all hunted seals and walruses from the sea ice. A hunter traveled to the **floe edge**, the place where the sea ice meets open water. He found a seal hole and waited patiently for the seal to come up to breathe. Quickly, he speared the seal with his **harpoon**. If he killed the seal, he lifted it from the hole and prepared it for the trip home. Inuit used every part of the animal. Women made sealskins into clothing and *kamiit*. They turned seal blubber into oil for *qulliit*, stone lamps. The meat fed many people.

Seal Holes

To find a seal hole, Inuit look for air bubbles along the edges of the hole. Next, a hunter needs to know if the seal is at the hole or off swimming. He ties a hair to a piece of wood and floats it in the water. If the hair moves, the seal is under the water.

Many seal hunters still use the traditional weapon for hunting, the harpoon.

An Inuit hunter builds his own kayak.

The Thule and Inuit built skin boats, **kayaks** and *umiaqs*, and made harpoons to kill whales. They attached floats made of skin "balloons" to the harpoon line. The floats kept a speared whale from diving. If a whale could dive, he might get away or capsize the boat. Men had to cooperate to kill a whale. One man couldn't do it.

Everyone shared the whale meat and blubber. Elders decided who would get what parts. They thought about who needed food and who helped to kill the whale. Everyone celebrated. There would be food for a long time.

Inuit Guides—Rocks, Stars, and Snow

Inuit families needed to move from place to place, hunting and fishing in a large area. Dogsleds allowed them to move quickly across snow and ice. Travel was easiest in the winter, when sea ice and snow covered the Arctic. In spring and summer, open water and soggy ground made traveling difficult.

In the winter, it was dark most of the day and night. There were no roads, no road signs. Trails disappeared in blowing snow. The Inuit developed special methods to find their way across the land. They memorized landmarks and shorelines. Travelers built stone figures, *inuksuit*. Each *inuksuk* had a meaning. Many were direction markers. Some honored people or spirits. Some warned of danger. The Inuit used *inuksuit* like road signs.

During dark seasons, the Inuit sometimes navigated using stars. They also used the snow. The wind in the central Canadian Arctic usually blows from one direction. The wind creates piles of snow. The snow freezes and in the next storm, more is added. Hard ridges of snow, called **uqalurait**, run from northwest to southeast. Following the ridges leads to one direction. Crossing the ridges leads to another. One way or another, Inuit hunters found their way home.

Inuit call these seven stars Tukturjuit, *the Great Caribou (right). These stars are also called the Big Dipper (left).*

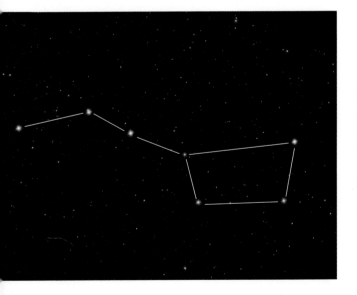

Children leave their summer tents to go out and play. The tents are a part of a fishing camp.

Chapter Three

Living on the Land

For generations, home was where the caribou traveled, where the seals surfaced, where berries grew. Whether their shelter was a summer tent or a winter igloo, Inuit children were told when they woke to "go out and see the world." Children started each day with a view of the land that fed and clothed them. They dressed, ate, and began their daily chores. The Inuit made everything they needed from the land. There was a lot to do.

Seasons on the Land

During summer, it was difficult and often dangerous to travel across soggy tundra. As the surface of the permafrost melts, sinkholes, or bottomless pits, can form on the tundra. Sometimes they are invisible and can trap travelers. The summer warmth also melts sea ice. However, the Inuit could travel by boat in the summer months.

Inuit families set up skin tents at summer camps. They settled in to fish and gather berries and eggs. They hunted geese and ducks. Women dried fish and sewed skins. Men hunted

The traditional summer tent has evolved over the years. This tent has a stove with a chimney.

beluga and bowhead whales and narwhals that were returning to the open waters.

As fall approached, hunters followed migrating caribou. Every caribou killed meant meat for the winter, blankets for igloos, and skins for parkas and wind pants. Women dried and scraped the skins. They preserved caribou and whale meat, and they rendered, or processed, blubber into oil for fuel.

In the winter, snow fell. The sea froze. Winds howled. The Inuit put away their tents and built igloos. The sod or snow houses were heated with burning seal or whale oil. They were warm.

Inuit hunters paid close attention to the weather. Anyone caught in a blizzard could be lost and freeze to death. If no storms threatened, the Inuit went hunting. Travel was easier in the winter because sea ice was solid and snow was hard. As days became shorter, men hunted seal or ice-fished in the dark. When the hunters didn't find game, people ate meat they had preserved during the summer. Sometimes they went hungry.

In the spring, the sea ice began to melt, and the floe edge came closer to shore. Spring was a good time to hunt seal and walrus at the floe edge. Hunters often cut up their kill on the ice and returned home with a sled piled with meat and sealskins. Elders divided the meat, and women dried and prepared the skins.

In the summer, snow melted and the tundra bloomed. Children played in flowery meadows late into the night. The Inuit moved to summer camps, set up their tents, and began the cycle again.

Rendering Blubber

One way to render seal blubber into oil is to cut it into chunks. Put the chunks in a pail for a few days at about 40° F (4.4°C). Stir them each day. Soon the blubber will turn to oil.

The Floe Edge

The floe edge makes a dark reflection in the sky. As the floe edge moves closer to land, the reflection moves higher in the sky.

Working Together

In Inuit tradition, men hunted the game that fed and clothed the community. They drove the dog teams, decided when the ice was safe for travel, and built igloos. To build a snow igloo, they chose a place protected from the weather and found the right snow for cutting snow blocks. Hunters used their long knives to cut the blocks. They dug the entrance tunnel lower than the igloo's floor. Cold air sank into the tunnel while warm air filled the house.

Women cared for the children and tended the *qulliit*, or oil lamps, that warmed Inuit homes. They prepared and preserved food. Women scraped and softened animal skins and sewed them into clothing that kept everyone warm and alive in extreme cold. A good seamstress protected her family. If a man froze his fingers or toes, people said his wife was bad at sewing!

Two men work together to build an igloo. Using a saw, they cut the snow into blocks.

Children didn't go to school. They learned from their families. Children learned to share, be patient, and be observant. The Inuit said watching was the best way to learn. Girls watched their mothers sew. They might chew a piece of sealskin to soften it or scrape hair from bearded seal hide for a *kamik* sole. A girl's first sewing project might be making a pair of mitts for her father, little *kamiit* to protect the dogs' feet from the ice, or clothes for her doll.

Boys watched their fathers make tools. They might have their own small tools. Boys hunted with their fathers or grandfathers. They learned where to find game and how to use a spear and a harpoon. Everyone celebrated a child's first successful hunt. The Inuit expected children to have the skills to care for a family before they married.

A Community for Life

Life in the Arctic is dangerous. A hunter could fall through the ice or be attacked by a polar bear. No one knew when the next seal or caribou would be killed. The Inuit survived because they had close relationships with many people and because they shared. Traditions helped adults and children know their responsibilities to their family and community.

Elders had a lifetime of knowledge. They passed down history, legends, beliefs, and practical knowledge. They told the stories of their youth. They had learned how people worked best together, how the weather changed, where animals traveled. Elders helped choose husbands and wives, name babies,

Celebrating a First Hunt

Inuit people often remember important moments with poems or songs. This poem, written by one of the Aivilik Inuit, proudly tells of a boy's first hunt:

On his very first hunt
He killed a fine seal
Even in the dark.

An Inuit girl helps her grandmother cut fish. Inuit families work together to help each other.

decide where to camp, and divide meat. Elders settled arguments in the community. Inuit children were taught to visit elders and help them. They had earned respect.

Shamans had spiritual powers. Tradition says shamans could change into animals, fly, or visit spirits underground or in the ocean. When someone was too sick to be helped with herbs or by other ordinary healing ways, a shaman was called to heal him. People gathered around to watch and hear the

24

shaman's instructions. Sometimes he told everyone to fast, or go without food, for a few days, or he gave the patient a special diet. Good shamans helped people. Bad ones could hurt them.

Men often became hunting partners. Partners traveled and hunted together. They protected and helped each other. Hunting partners shared food and cared for each other's families.

Parents chose their children's husbands and wives, often promising the baby to a future spouse at birth. A woman moved in with her husband's family when she married. If she was young, her mother-in-law helped her learn about caring for a family. Men were taught to care for their in-laws as they would their own parents. Parents and grandparents helped raise children.

Each baby had a ***sanariarruk***, someone who pledged to help the child grow into a good man or woman. A boy brought the first animal he killed to his *sanariarruk*. A girl gave hers the first pieces she sewed. Some babies were adopted by relatives or friends. Often grandparents adopted the first child of their oldest child. If a baby's parents were young or sick, elders could decide whether the child should be adopted.

The Inuit had many close relationships. They took care of each other. That was their way.

First Aid

The Inuit used caribou antlers for splints and dried caribou membranes for bandages. They knew how to use plants such as willow, yarrow, and rose hips for healing.

The arrival of outsiders to Inuit lands brought many changes for the Inuit people.

Chapter Four

Visitors Arrive

A hunter traveled quickly across the ice at the floe edge. He watched the ice for patterns that told him it was solid. He scanned the horizon, as he always did, looking for animals. Suddenly he signaled his dogs to stop. He squinted at the water. At first, he couldn't guess what he was seeing. Then he was sure he saw a boat, but it wasn't a kayak or an *umiaq*. It was big, pushed by huge white sails. The Inuit didn't build boats like this. Neither did the Indians he'd met while traveling in the south. The hunter wondered who was coming. What did they want?

A Handful of Europeans

Europeans had arrived. Dorset and Thule people in Greenland may have met Nordic European people who lived in southern Greenland between about 985 and the early 1400s. Basque whalers and fishermen, from today's Spain and France, probably landed in Labrador in the 1500s.

In 1576, English explorer Martin Frobisher searched for a new sea route to China. At that time, people believed there must be a way to sail to China by going north of North America—the Northwest Passage. He sailed from Greenland to Baffin Island and northern Labrador. He returned two years later with fifteen ships and a hundred settlers to begin an English colony. However, extreme cold forced them to return to England.

John Davis sailed to Baffin Island in 1585, 1586, and 1587. He reported seeing large numbers of whales. Henry Hudson explored arctic waters in 1610. Hudson's ship was trapped by sea ice. He and his crew spent the winter on the shore of what is known now as Hudson Bay. In the spring, the crew rebelled. They put Hudson, his son, and a few men in a small boat, took the sailing ship, and started back to England. Hudson was never found.

Other explorers followed. They didn't know the Arctic Ocean was frozen year-round. Finally, Norway's Roald Amundsen led an expedition that navigated the Northwest Passage between 1903 and 1906.

From Whaling Crews to Flight Crews

Europeans, or *qallunaat*, were not prepared to live in the Arctic. The few who dared were whalers, trappers, and traders. Although some explorers were killed by the Inuit, most Inuit helped the visitors. They helped Europeans stay warm. They guided them from place to place. Inuit taught the Europeans how to dress in Inuit clothing and use dogsleds.

As the south filled with European settlers, the Inuit were mostly left alone. Beginning in the mid-1800s, Scottish and American whalers sailed arctic seas. Whale oil was used for fuel, whalebone for support in ladies' underwear and other things. The whalers set up camps and hired Inuit whalers. The Inuit knew the seas. They knew where to find whales. They were used to the cold and were fine whale hunters.

During the late 1800s, some Inuit worked in the whaling camps. They spent their earnings on goods such as tea, flour,

This engraving shows whalers at work.

guns, ammunition, and cooking pots. They ate bannock, a Scottish fried bread, and drank tea. They learned Scottish songs and dances. Some Inuit women married European men.

Whalers brought some things to the north for the first time. They had books and written language. They followed Christian religions. Some whalers carried European diseases such as measles and smallpox. The Inuit's bodies often were not able to fight off the new diseases. Whalers drank alcohol, which was also new to the Inuit.

Whalers killed thousands of arctic whales every year. By the beginning of the 1900s, it was hard to find bowhead whales. Whalers abandoned their arctic towns. However, the Inuit still wanted to buy southern goods.

In the early 1900s, the Hudson's Bay Company built trading posts in the Canadian Arctic to buy fox skins and sealskins from Inuit and Indian trappers. The Inuit, who had gathered at whaling stations, now scattered in small groups to trap foxes and seals. Many Inuit families did well trapping for Hudson's Bay. Some purchased things such as boats for summer fishing and rifles for hunting.

By the mid-1900s, only a few southern Canadians and Americans lived in the Arctic. Some were missionaries. They settled at trading posts to convert the Inuit to Christianity. Many Inuit became Catholics. Others accepted the Anglican faith. The Inuit began to use the Christian calendar and to celebrate Christian holidays such as Christmas. Missionaries taught the Inuit that they should not hunt or travel on Sunday.

Beluga Whales

Today about 50,000 to 70,000 beluga whales live in arctic waters. Inuit hunters kill about 600 to 700 a year. They use every part of the whale. In the late 1800s, Scottish whalers trapped hundreds of belugas at a time, butchering them on the beach for their oil and bone.

A day without travel often meant going hungry, but the Inuit honored the Christian tradition.

When the United States entered World War II, in 1941, the U.S. and Canadian governments built military bases in Alaska, northern Canada, and Greenland. Many Inuit came to the bases to trade or to work. With more people living close together, it was easier for diseases, such as tuberculosis, to spread across the Arctic.

After the war, some bases closed. During the 1950s, however, Canada and the United States built other military projects such as the Distant Early Warning Line, a line of radar stations near the Arctic Circle. The Inuit continued to live on the land. Missionaries and the Canadian government built schools in the trading settlements. The Canadian government opened nursing stations to treat diseases and to immunize children.

The Hudson's Bay Company still exists today. This photograph shows one of the company's buildings in Panignitung.

Settlements—Good and Bad

At the end of the 1950s, the Canadian government wanted to settle Inuit families in southern-style towns. Many Inuit were starving. The caribou they depended on had not returned as usual. Other Inuit were dying of diseases spread from the military bases and installations. Canadian officials wanted Inuit children to go to school. They wanted them to learn to read and write English or French.

In the late 1950s, diseases and diminished food supplies caused much suffering for the Inuit.

When the Inuit were on the land, officials didn't know where or how many Inuit there were. At that time, the Canadian government identified Inuit people by numbers instead of names. The Canadian government wanted firm control of the Arctic. Few southern Canadians wanted to move there. Inuit settlements would be new Canadian towns.

However, many Inuit wanted to stay on the land. The government placed Inuit children in residential schools. At the schools, children learned to read and write in English or French, and Inuktitut. They got medical care. However, they had to live away from their families and get used to a strange way of life. Sometimes they were treated badly by the school staff.

Many Inuit parents finally settled in towns to be near their children. The southern-style houses couldn't be heated with whale or seal oil. There wasn't enough game for all the people settled in the communities. Now the Inuit had to have jobs to buy the food and fuel they needed. However, older Inuit did not speak English or French. Younger people had been raised to be hunters, not employees. They planned their days by the weather, not by the Canadian calendar. Sometimes men went hunting during good weather instead of going to work. Then they could lose their jobs.

In the settlements, some Inuit were able to earn money. They bought snowmobiles, which were cheaper to keep up and faster than dogsleds. Women bought prepared threads and fabrics. Children went to school. Some families prospered. Others struggled.

In the 1960s, the Canadian government shot hundreds of sled dogs. The government said they were destroyed to prevent disease. Without their dogs, many Inuit could not hunt.

The Inuit could get alcohol in the settlements. Some became alcoholics. Many Inuit felt their language and traditions were being lost. They wanted their children to speak more Inuktitut. They wanted more time together to pass on the stories and skills that had made Inuit successful for centuries. They wanted change.

Snowmobiles remain a popular way for the Inuit to get around.

An elderly Inuit man drum sings using the traditional drum.

Chapter Five

Keeping Traditions

Today many Inuit gather at special occasions for drum dances. A drummer may sway back and forth, beating a skin drum as he begins his song. He sings a *pisiq*, or verse, telling a story about his life. Women accompany singing *"a-ja-ja-a."* The drummer might tell a hunting story and then sing a song teasing a friend. When he is done, he hands the drum to a young woman. She is the next drummer. It is disrespectful to refuse the drum. Each drummer sings a different song. The song might be made up right then, or it might be one that the drummer sings often. Drummers pick songs to fit the moment.

Good Reasons for Fun

The Inuit did not have a written language. Songs and stories were passed by memory. A good storyteller makes his story come alive. He often begins, "I will tell it as it was told to me, I will not alter it." Many stories are funny—humor is important to the Inuit. Sometimes they are brutally honest. Often there is something in a story to learn.

In the past, a song was a treasured possession. Each singer had his own songs that he "owned." However, others might remember them and retell them. **Drum dancing** helped people remember their past. Sometimes people used their verses to argue with or insult each other. They drummed instead of

fighting. Inuit still enjoy drum dancing for entertainment or special occasions. Today Inuit children may practice drum dancing at school.

A young boy practices a traditional drum dance at school.

Schoolchildren also learn traditional stories, myths, and games. Winter was the season for string games. The Inuit used a long loop of string to make figures such as caribou, huts, and kayaks. Drop a loop and the caribou moved or the kayak capsized!

A teacher shows his students how to play string games.

A young Inupiat Inuit boy jumps during a whaling feast.

Ballplayers in the Sky

Inuit legend says some souls go to live in the sky when they die. The **northern lights** are paths the spirits make when they play ball. Their ball is a walrus head. If the lights get too close to people on Earth, the ball can knock their heads off! Whistle, and the lights move closer. If you are scared, rub your fingernails together, and the lights move away.

Hunters needed to keep their muscles strong and their reflexes quick during long, dark days inside. Many traditional Inuit games were played in the space inside the igloo. Men wrestled, pulled each other's fingers and ears, and kicked targets hung from the ceiling. The winners were strong and quick and could stand pain. In northern Alaska, whole communities were divided into two ball teams. A baby was assigned his team at birth. Everyone played a soccerlike game at special occasions and festivals.

Today, northern communities hold races, games, and drum dances during community festivals and holidays. At these times, people wear traditional clothing. They may wear a treasured parka made by an ancestor or a new piece sewn specially for them.

Sewing: Women's Art

Many Inuit women sew the parkas and wind pants for their families. They make ***amautiit***, the hooded parkas mothers use to carry their babies. They decorate children's parkas with emblems of their favorite ice hockey team, arctic animals, or cartoon characters. Although not all of today's Inuit women know how to work with skins, many do. Older women teach younger women to make mitts, parkas, and *kamiit*.

Sealskin is prepared by soaking it in water, salt, and detergent. For a white color, women dip the skins in hot water and scrape the fur off. They roll, stomp, squash, and chew the skin to soften it. Sometimes skins are squeezed in a "modern invention"—huge plastic teeth mounted on hinged pieces of wood.

Women make paper patterns for cutting the pieces. The seamstress uses an ***ulu***, or a woman's knife with a half-moon shaped blade, to shave the edges of the skin so the seams won't be bulky. Now she is ready to sew. If she is making *kamiit*, she will use special tiny stitches to make the soles waterproof. The piece will be a work of art, made for a special person.

The hood of the amauti keeps a child warm and close to his or her mother.

Kamiit Custom

When someone is bundled up from head to toe in a parka, wind pants, and *kamiit*, it can be hard to tell if that person is a man or a woman. Traditionally, Inuit sew men's and women's *kamiit* in different ways. Men's *kamiit* are sewn so that the hairs of the fur point up and down the man's leg. Women's *kamiit* are made with the hairs pointing sideways around the woman's leg. That way, you can look people's *kamiit* and know if they are men or women!

This is an Inuit wall hanging.

Women also use their sewing skills to make wall hangings. They piece bright-colored felt into scenes from the north. Polar bears may dance around an igloo, or Inuit may ice-fish, seal hunt, and sled across the background. Women design and stitch stunning art.

World-Class Artists

Traditional Inuit were taught to remember the details they saw in the land. They had to predict weather, remember directions, and track game using what they saw. Today many Inuit use the same skills to produce art. They carve stones into bears, walruses, or caribou. They make prints of drum dancers, shamans, and mythical creatures.

Although much Inuit art shows traditional stories and animals, today's art is different from older Inuit work. In the past, Inuit carved small pieces of soapstone, bone, or ivory. Anything they made had to be carried from place to place, so art usually decorated something useful. Today's Inuit sculptors carve many kinds of stones and bone. The finished pieces may be tiny or quite large.

Inuit drawings and prints are fairly new. In the 1950s, a group in Cape Dorset, encouraged by southerner, James Houston, began making prints to sell in the south. Today their West Baffin Eskimo Co-op is famous for its fine artwork. Other communities are known for their art too. In some towns, almost all the adults earn some of their living by selling art. Inuit art is sold in galleries around the world. Drawings of stories told at drum dances might hang in offices in New York or in living rooms in Paris.

An artist works on a soapstone carving of different animal forms.

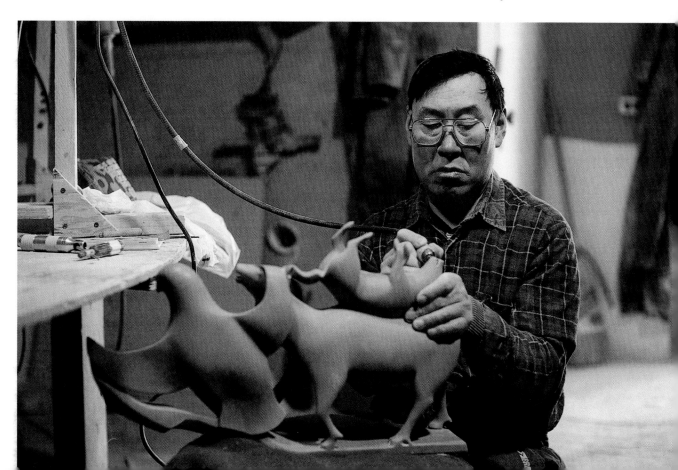

A young man participates in the two foot high kick at the Arctic Winter Games.

Chapter Six

Walking Forward, Looking Back

A boy starts in the corner of the gym. He lies flat, then pushes himself up on his wrists and toes. Holding his body stiff above the floor, he hops to the center of the floor. The crowd cheers. He's just won the seal hop! Next, contestants take turns at the Alaska high kick. A target, called the seal, is hung from the ceiling. One at a time, each athlete sits on the

Two Foot High Kick

Unlike the Alaska high kick, the people who participate in the two foot high kick take off and land with both feet. This allows them to jump even higher.

floor beneath the seal and grabs one foot with the opposite hand. High kickers use their free hand to support themselves as they kick at the seal with the foot they aren't holding. The seal is raised again and again. The person who kicks it when it's highest wins. A winning Alaska high kick can be 7 feet (2.1 m).

The athletes are at the **Arctic Winter Games**, where teams from around the Arctic compete in traditional Inuit and Native American games. They play indoor soccer, basketball, curling, and ice hockey too. Young athletes from Greenland, Alaska, Siberia, and northern Canada have trained for two years for these events. Their families and friends cheer them on in English, French, Russian, Danish, and Inuktitut.

Kids whose grandparents were born in tents and igloos have come by jet to an athletic event fashioned after ancient Greek games. They wear tennis shoes made in Singapore, jeans from the United States, and parkas sewn by their mothers. They snack on *kukuks*, or chocolates, and caribou jerky. They will dance one night to their favorite rock music. The next night they'll square-dance and reel to Scottish and American folk tunes until the floor bounces and rumbles.

Old and New—a Balancing Act

Life in the north has changed quickly during the last fifty years. Southern education, communication, and travel have opened the world to the Inuit. Inuit students have drum danced in Japan and on the same piers in Scotland where whalers departed for arctic waters a hundred years ago. Some

Inuit are college professors, Royal Canadian Mounted Police officers, and company presidents.

However, to some, the changes have been confusing. Northern communities have high rates of alcoholism and suicide. Jobs can be hard to find. Although most Inuit hunt for part of their food, they must buy some too. They have electric and gasoline bills. They need snowmobiles and guns. In the north, prices are high. Food and supplies must be flown in or barged in during the short summer. Many families don't have enough money.

Many Inuit children go to school near their homes. However, others must live away from home to attend high school or community college. The closest universities are hundreds of miles to the south. For Inuit students, used to living in communities of close family and friends, studying away from home can be very lonely.

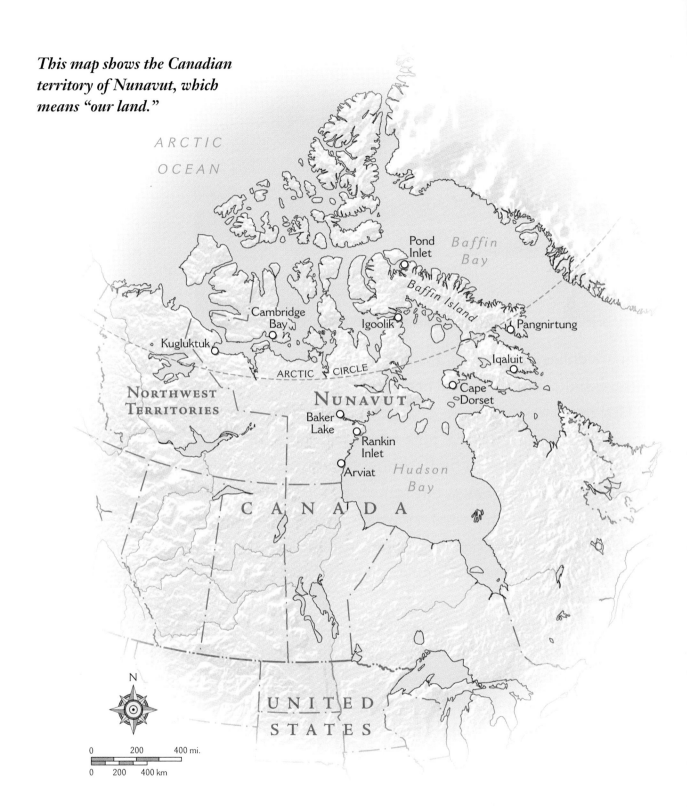

This map shows the Canadian territory of Nunavut, which means "our land."

ARCTIC
OCEAN

*Baffin
Bay*

Pond
Inlet

Baffin Island

Cambridge
Bay

Igoolik

Pangnirtung

Kugluktuk

ARCTIC CIRCLE

Iqaluit

NORTHWEST
TERRITORIES

NUNAVUT

Cape
Dorset

Baker
Lake

Rankin
Inlet

Arviat

*Hudson
Bay*

C A N A D A

N

UNITED
STATES

0   200   400 mi.

0   200   400 km

Our Land, Nunavut

Few Inuit want to return to living only in traditional ways. However, most want to preserve Inuit skills, language, and values. As southerners took more and more control of Inuit life, many Inuit felt they were losing their own land. Legal claims were filed saying much of the north belonged to the Inuit, not to Canada. In 1979, the **Inuit Tapiriiksat**, a group of politically active Inuit leaders, proposed a way to settle the land claims. Part of their solution was to create a new Canadian territory, Nunavut.

After years of negotiating and voting, Nunavut, which means "our land," became a territory on April 1, 1999. In 2002, about 85 percent of its 28,000 people were Inuit or other native people. The people of Nunavut are Canadians. However, Inuit and other northerners are now managing their own land and resources. The Inuit are proud that they gained control of their homeland without violence. The Inuit in other parts of Canada are waiting to settle their claims. In the meantime, the creation of Nunavut is admired by native people around the world.

Today's Inuit are connected to the world by Internet and jet. They are also connected by the land and sea they love. Pollution created in faraway places reaches the Arctic. Chemicals arrive in ocean and air currents. Air pollution from the south settles with the cold air that sinks over the Arctic. Arctic cold keeps garbage and pollutants from decomposing as they would in warmer climates. Arctic pollution takes years to break down.

Scientists are studying how global warming might change

the Arctic. Animals may change their migration routes. Weather may be harsher. The ice pack may shrink. The **Inuit Circumpolar Conference** encourages arctic research by and with Inuit people. Politicians from southern countries, who make decisions that affect the Arctic, may never have been north. The group stands up for the Arctic to the rest of the world. Inuit once protected European, Canadian, and American explorers. Today they are preserving their traditions, protecting their land, and speaking for our earth.

Inuit believe the present is connected to the past. Inuit tradition says a spirit lives on with a person's name. When a loved one dies, a new baby will be named for that person. People believe the baby will be like their loved one. The baby "inherits" a set of friends and relatives along with his name. He has a ready-made place in people's hearts. The child already knows and loves the land.

Inuit children carry on the traditions and the spirits of their ancestors. When today's children drum their songs, it is the words of their people that they sing. They learn stories that they may tell to their children, "as it was told to me." When they share *maktaaq*, skin, from a bowhead whale hunt, they honor the tradition of their grandparents and great-grandparents. When they graduate from university, win a place at the Arctic Winter Games, or learn to fly a jet, they have with them the pride of loved ones and the hopes of those at home. They are the past and the future of the Inuit.

Timeline

Before 10,000 B.C.	Bering Land Bridge allows migration of Asian people to North America.
8000–5000 B.C	Paleo-Arctic people live in Alaska and Yukon.
2200–800 B.C	Arctic Small Tool tradition is present in Alaska and Canada.
About 500 B.C	Dorset culture develops in the Canadian Arctic. Thule culture develops in Alaska.
About A.D. 1 –1000	Thule culture spreads east from Alaska to as far west as Greenland.
985–1408	Norse people live in settlements in Greenland.
1500s	Basque fishermen and whalers sail near Labrador.
1576	Martin Frobisher searches for the Northwest Passage.
1585–1587	John Davis explores arctic waters.
1610	Henry Hudson explores Hudson Bay.
1850s–1920s	Scottish and American whalers are active in the Arctic.
1870	Canada acquires traditional Inuit lands.
Early 1900s	Hudson's Bay Company establishes trading posts in the Canadian Arctic.
Mid-1900s	Missionaries and governments set up residential schools.

continued next page

49

Timeline *continued*

1941–1950s	United States and Canada build military bases in the Arctic.
1950s	Caribou fail to return on usual routes.
1951–1962	James Houston encourages Inuit artists in Cape Dorset. West Baffin Eskimo Co-op is established.
1950s–1970s	Inuit are encouraged to live in settlements.
1970	First Arctic Winter Games are held in Yellowknife, Northwest Territories, Canada.
1979	Inuit Tapiriiksat proposes a settlement of land claims against Canadian government.
1992	The Canadian government and Inuit adopt a plan to settle land claims and create the territory Nunavut.
1999	Nunavut becomes a Canadian territory.

Glossary

adapted—changed to be better able to live in a particular type of place

amauti—a jacket with a large hood that women use to carry a baby

Arctic Small Tool tradition—the prehistoric arctic culture known for its fine stone tools

Arctic Winter Games—an athletic competition for arctic youth, held every two years

axis—a line around which things turn

Bering Land Bridge—an ancient land bridge between Asia and North America

blubber—a thick layer of fat on a marine animal

Dorset—an early culture centered in the Canadian Arctic

drum dancing—a traditional art form, in which a drummer sings or tells a story and moves to the beat of his drum

elder—a respected older member of the community

floe edge—a place where sea ice meets open water

harpoon—a special spear, connected to a line

hibernate—to sleep through the winter

igloo—a house traditionally made of sod, snow, or ice blocks

Inuit Circumpolar Conference—a political group that represents Inuit from around the world

Inuit Tapiriiksat—a group that works for Inuit causes

inuksuk—a group of stones that act like a person, giving directions, warnings, and other messages

Inuktitut—the language spoken by central and eastern Canadian Inuit

kamik—a waterproof boot made of seal or other skin

kayak—a small traditional skin boat

kukuk—chocolate

maktaaq—strips of whale skin that are eaten

migrate—to travel, usually moving with the seasons

northern lights—moving colored lights that sometimes appear in the Arctic night sky

Nunavut—is Inuit for "our land." It is a Canadian territory on traditionally Inuit land.

Paleo-Arctic people—the earliest people known to have lived in the Arctic

parka—a long hooded jacket

permafrost—a layer of ground that is frozen year-round

pisiq—a verse of a drum song

precipitation—any form of water that falls, such as rain or snow

qallunaat—the Inuit name for white people

qulliit—traditional stone lamps used to heat igloos and tents

rotate—to turn in a circle

sanariarruk—a person who promises to teach and protect a child

shaman—a person who is believed to be able to visit spirits, do magic, and heal illness

southern—a term for people and things from European, Canadian, and American cultures

string games—traditional games of creating figures with a loop of string

Thule—an early culture that began in northwest Alaska and spread as far as Greenland

tundra—area of low-growing plants that grow in short summers on wet ground

Tuniit—an Inuit name for people who lived on their land before them

tupiq—a traditional skin tent

ulu—a traditional woman's knife with a half-moon shaped blade

umiaq—a large traditional skin boat

uqalurait—snow ridges that can be used to tell directions

To Find Out More

Books

Brimner, Larry Dane. *Polar Mammals.* Danbury, Connecticut: Children's Press, 1999.

Kittredge, Frances. *Neeluk: An Eskimo Boy in the Days of the Whaling Ships.* Anchorage: Alaska Northwest Books, 2001.

Kusagak, Michael Arvaarluk. *Arctic Stories.* Toronto: Annick Press Ltd.,1998.

Lutz, Norma Jean. *Nunavut: Canada in the 21st Century.* New York: Chelsea House, 2001.

Senungetuk, Vivian and Tiulana, Paul. *Place for Winter; Wise Words of Paul Tiulana: An Inupiat Alaskan's Life.* Danbury Connecticut: Franklin Watts, 1999.

Tookoome, Simon with Oberman, Sheldon. *The Shaman's Nephew: A Life in the Far North*. Toronto: Stoddart Kids, 1999.

Wallace, Mary. *The Inuksuk Book*. Toronto: Owl Books, 1999.

Organizations and Online Sites

Aboriginal Canada Portal
http://www.aboriginalcanada.gc.ca/abdt/interface/interface2.nsf/engdoc/0.html
This is a site about Canada's First Nations, including Inuit people. Click on "Kids" for legends, games, languages, and photos.

Alaska Native Heritage Center
8800 Heritage Center Drive
Anchorage, Alaska 99506
The Alaska Native Heritage Center shares and celebrates Alaska Native cultures.

Cape Dorset Inuit Art and Inuit Cultural Perspectives
http://collections.ic.gc.ca/cape_dorset/index2.html
The site features Inuit art and interviews with Inuit elders about traditional skills.

The Government of Nunavut
http://www.gov.nu.ca
This site provides information and contacts for the territorial government.

Indian and Northern Affairs Canada
http://www.ainc-inac.gc.ca/ks/index_e.html
Click on Kids' Stop to hear phrases in Inuktitut and read articles about aboriginal people, Nunavut, and Northwest Territories.

Inuit Circumpolar Conference
170 Laurier, Suite 504
Ottawa, Ontario K1P 5V5
http://www.inuitcircumpolar.com
The Inuit Circumpolar Conference addresses scientific and political issues that are important to arctic people around the world.

Inuit Tapiriit Kanatami
170 Laurier, Suite 510
Ottawa, Ontario K1P 5V5
http://www.itk.ca
This is the national Inuit organization of Canada. The site has information on Inuit culture and history.

Nunavut Handbook
http://www.arctic-travel.com
Nunavut Handbook has information on Inuit culture, history, art, music, games, and related subjects such as arctic communities, animals, and travel.

Online Classroom Expedition
http://www.arcticblast.polarhusky.com
Look here for information about all kinds of people, animals, and things in the arctic.

Tungasuvvingat Inuit, Ontario Inuit Center
http://www.ontarioinuit.ca
This site has links to history, games, dance groups, Inuktitut language, and other cultural information in the About Inuit section.

Virtual Museum of Canada
http://www.virtualmusuem.ca
The Virtual Museum of Canada has images, information, and classroom resources online from many Canadian museums. Search "Inuit" to find online exhibits.

Windspeaker, Online Classroom Editions
http://www.ammsa.com/classroom/
Windspeaker is an online magazine featuring articles by and about Canadian First Nations and Inuit people.

A Note on Sources

To research *The Inuit*, I read many books and searched for and read articles on the Internet. Then I traveled to Rankin Inlet, Nunavut, Canada, to meet Inuit people. I interviewed students at Maani Ulujuk Ilinniarvik (Middle School) about hunting on the land, visiting friends and relatives, and their favorite things to do in town. They demonstrated traditional Inuit games and taught me some Inuktitut. Four students from Bev Hill's class, Emelda Aupilardjuk, Krista Passeor, Joe Patterk, and Moses Sanertanut, were especially helpful. Helen Iguptak, the Inuit culture and Inuktitut instructor at Maani Ulujuk shared her thoughts, her bannock, and her books with me. The people of Rankin Inlet are my most important resource in writing this book. I learned more from watching and listening to them than I could from any book.

Not everyone can go to Nunavut, so, luckily, there are books to read. An adult book I'd recommend is *Saqiyuq: Stories from the Lives of Three Inuit Women* by Nancy Wachowich, Apphia Agalakti Awa, Rhoda Kaukjak Katsuk, and Sandra Pikujak Katsuk. *Saqiyuq* is written from interviews with a grandmother, a mother, and a daughter. Their stories of growing up at different times in the last century reflect the huge changes Inuit have experienced since the 1950s. Two other useful books on specific Inuit traditions are *The Arctic Sky, Inuit Astronomy, Star Lore and Legend* by John MacDonald and *Our Boots: An Inuit Women's Art* by Jill Oakes and Rick Riewe. Both these books share information gathered from Inuit elders, legends, and the personal experiences of the authors. For a photographer's view of inuksuit, along with thorough information on them, read *Inuksuit: Silent Messengers of the North* by Norman Hallendy.

I found good information in children's books too. *The Shaman's Nephew: A Life in the Far North* by Simon Tookoome with Sheldon Oberman uses Tookoome's art and stories to tell about his life on the land and moving into a settlement. Michael Arvaarluk Kusagak's numerous picture books bring Inuit legends and his own memories to life.

When I was on the web, although I used many sites, I returned over and over to the Nunavut Handbook at http://www.arctictravel.com. This book-length site is packed with information about the Arctic, Inuit, travel, and history. If you can't go to Nunavut in person, this site will take you on a virtual tour online.

—*Suzanne M. Williams*

Index

Numbers in *italics* indicate illustrations.

About the Author

Suzanne M. Williams has a B.A. from University of California, Davis, a M.Ed. from College of Notre Dame, Belmont, California, and an A.M.S. Montessori Certificate, and holds state teaching credentials. For Scholastic Library Publishing, she has written *Kentucky* and *Nevada* for Sea to Shining Sea, Second Series. She is also the author of *Made in China, Ideas and Inventions from Ancient China, Piñatas and Smiling Skeletons, Celebrating Mexican Festivals*, and other non-fiction children's books.